With My Profound Reverence for the Victims

GEORGE BELLOWS

August 13 - September 23

2001

SAMUEL DORSKY MUSEUM OF ART

STATE UNIVERSITY OF NEW YORK

NEW PALTZ

Preface

A Fortuitous Confluence of Events

The lithographer's art dates back to the late 18th century with the invention of a printing process by Aloys Senefelder in 1796, based on the transfer of a drawing on stone to paper. Although it was originally developed as a commercial reproductive process, from its inception, artists in Europe immediately employed the technique for expressive and creative purposes. In 1917 a group of artists in the United States founded an organization called the Painter-Gravers of America. The organization included many of the leading artists of the time and was dedicated to securing recognition of the fine print as a viable medium of creative expression. The group, headed by Albert Sterner, included George Bellows, Childe Hassam, Boardman Robinson, and John Sloan, among others.[1] George Bellows' deep commitment to lithography as an expressive medium can be dated to the founding of the group and continued throughout his life. Although Bellows is best known for his paintings of city life and sporting events, in particular boxing matches, he specifically chose printmaking as the medium to use in order to come to terms with the social and political realities of his time that concerned him so deeply.

The art of lithography is generally a collaborative effort between the artist and the printer. It is the printer's responsibility to convey the spirit of the artist's intent from the drawing made on stone, to the finished product. This is accomplished by a decision-making process that includes choices about the kind of crayon to use, the grinding of the stone, the kind and amount of ink to use, how much pressure the press exerts, and the type of paper selected. When George Bellows first began making lithographs, there were few printers in the country capable of true artistic collaboration. George Miller in New York City printed Bellows' earliest lithographs, but it was Bolton Coit Brown, one of the founders of the Byrdcliffe arts and crafts colony in Woodstock, New York (1902), and a seminal figure in the history of American lithography, who became Bellows' preferred printer.[2] Brown, a master technician and draftsman, dedicated his life as an artist to using and promoting lithography as an expressive medium. Together, Bellows and Brown developed a unique working relationship and a strong friendship. It was Brown who convinced Bellows of the superiority of printing directly from stone over the more facile and popular transfer process.[3] Bellows and Brown shared an uncommon passion for lithography, and working together they pushed the medium to its expressive limits.

Although Bellows lived and worked primarily in New York City, beginning 1920 he spent his summers and part of each fall at Woodstock in the heart of the Catskill Mountains. By that time, he was considered one of the most important lithographers in the country, and his prints were compared favorably with those of Daumier and Goya.[4] It was in Woodstock that Bellows' personal and professional relationship with Brown flourished.

A fortuitous confluence of events led to the development of this publication and the exhibition of lithographs by George Bellows that it documents. The Samuel Dorsky Museum of Art (SDMA), comprising the former SUNY New Paltz College Art Gallery (founded in 1964)[5] and a 9,000 square-foot addition, opened its doors to the public in April 2001. Its mission, though somewhat broad-based, includes a special commitment to address the rich cultural heritage of the Hudson Valley and Catskill regions. While the museum was still under construction, I became acquainted with a unique collection of work by artists associated with the historic Woodstock Art Colony, developed at Morgan Anderson Consulting in New York City. It was there that I first met Arthur A. Anderson, a passionate and informed collector whose incisive vision has guided and shaped that collection in a pointed and personal way. A center-piece of the collection is a comprehensive selection of works on paper by George Bellows, including the *War Series* a suite of prints created in response to reports that he read describing the German invasion of Belgium in 1915. When I first saw prints from the *War Series* they left me speechless, both for their content and their graphic power.

When the theme for the 2001 *Arts Now* biennial conference[6] at SUNY New Paltz was announced—*Sites of Conflict: Art in a Culture of Violence*—I immediately thought about Bellows' *War Series* and the possibility of developing an exhibition to add historic context to the symposium. Further inquiry into Bellows' work as a lithographer revealed that he created additional images that reflected on the theme of violence in the United States. The exhibition that I had originally envisioned begged to be expanded.

A call made at the suggestion of Arthur Anderson, to enlist the curatorial assistance of Glenn Peck of H. V. Allison and Company provided the project's missing link.[7] Peck, an impressive scholar, has dedicated the last 27 years of his career studying the life and work of George Bellows. In 1983 Peck and his colleague Gordon K. Allison, wrote an informative essay, "George Bellows and the War Series of 1918" in a catalogue for an exhibition held at Hirschl and Adler Galleries, New York.[8] I contacted Glenn Peck to seek his permission to reprint his essay in our catalogue. Peck suggested that I consider expanding the exhibition to include the prints that I had discovered in my research and offered to write a new essay specific to our exhibition and the conference. He also informed me that Arthur Anderson could provide the rest of the prints that I needed for the exhibition.

It is assumed that most of the prints in the *War Series* were made by Edward Krause, but Bolton Brown pulled at least one of them, and certainly a few of the other impressions in our exhibition. This catalogue reproduces the complete *War Series*, two war-related prints done after the series, and a selection of six prints created by Bellows in response to violence in American culture during the early 20th century. The prints provide insight into the artist's drafting and printmaking skills as well as his social conscience.

The opening of the Samuel Dorsky Museum of Art, the profound and haunting impact of the lithographs that I first saw in the collection at Morgan Anderson Consulting, a conference on art and violence, and encounters with two remarkable men, created the synergy that produced this publication and a profound and provocative exhibition. That it includes work done collaboratively by artists associated with the historic Woodstock Art Colony, gives the exhibition and the publication special importance to the museum.

I extend my personal gratitude to Arthur A. Anderson for his friendship, support, for his indefatigable efforts to develop a comprehensive collection of important work by artists associated with the historic Woodstock Art Colony, and for the irrepressible enthusiasm and generosity that enables him to willingly share that collection. Special thanks to Glenn Peck of H.V. Allison Company, who brings to the project a critically focused analysis that not only links it closely to the *Arts Now* conference but also enables the project to stand alone on its singular merit. I am grateful to Patricia C. Phillips, Dean of the School of Fine and Performing Arts, for her dedicated leadership and steadfast support of the SDMA. I express my appreciation and thanks to Mary Kastner and Laura Kniffen in the Publications Office, for the planning and design of the catalogue, and to Christine DeLape for her insightful editorial services and advice. I am indebted to the staff of the Samuel Dorsky Museum of Art: Cynthia Dill, Wayne Lempka, and Nadine Wasserman, for their dedication and tireless efforts that continue to ensure the high quality of our exhibitions and public programs.

The funding for this publication and for the exhibition was provided by a grant from the Dorsky Foundation. The Foundation's ongoing support of the SDMA helps to create the margin of excellence that we aspire to in all of our programs. Accordingly, I extend my sincerest gratitude to Karen, David, and Noah, and Sara Dorsky. This publication and the exhibition are dedicated to the memory of their father, and my friend, Samuel Dorsky.

Neil C. Trager, Director
Samuel Dorsky Museum of Art

[1] Clinton Adams, *Printmaking In New Mexico 1880–1990,* University of New Mexico, Albuquerque, NM, 1991 pp. 3- 4.

[2] Clinton Adams, *Crayonstone, The Life and Work of Bolton Brown, With a Catalogue of His Lithographs,* University of New Mexico, Albuquerque, NM, 1993. Brown began printing for Bellows in December 1918 or early 1919.

[3] A transfer lithograph is a lithograph drawn on one surface, usually paper, then transferred to another, generally zinc or stone, and then printed. Lithographs created by the process invented by Aloys Senefeleder are made from drawings created directly on the printing stone.

[4] Warren Adelson, *George Bellows Lithographs,* Adelson Galeries/Meredith Long & Company, n.d.

[5] For a history of the College Art Gallery see-*30-An Anniversary Exhibition*, College Art Gallery, SUNY New Paltz, 1994.

[6] SUNY New Paltz *Arts Now* conference, September 20-22, 2001.

[7] H.V. Allison & Co. are the exclusive representatives of the estate of George Bellows.

[8] Glenn C. Peck and Gordon K. Allison, *George Bellows and the War Series of 1918,* Hirshl & Adler Galleries, Inc, NY, 1983. The exhibition was held from March 19 – April 16, 1983, and traveled to the Museum of Fine Arts in Springfield, Massachusetts, where it was on view from October 19 – December 4, 1983.

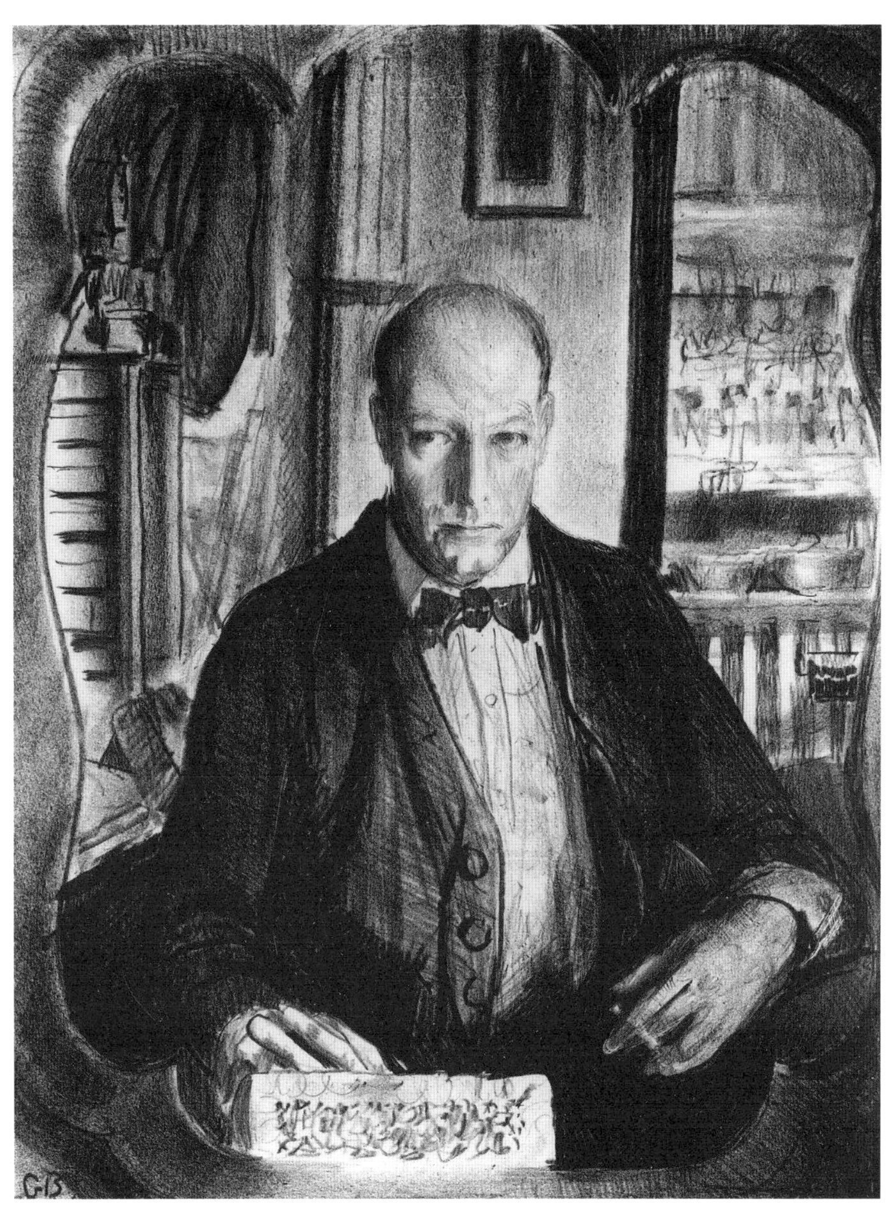

Self-Portrait, 1921
lithograph
10 ½ x 7 ⅞ inches

Does One Collect?

There was a time, not so long ago, when I didn't use the word "collector." It reminded me of when, as a boy in Michigan, I collected stamps or, later in college, when I collected old books, travel books in particular. From both I learned geography and history and traveled to far corners of the globe in my mind's eye. The pieces of postage paper came from where? And what previous owner had treasured my travel books? The emotional content of my collecting was the thrill of the chase, the discovery of something new and the patina of something old. These were indeed collections, a group of objects having a common theme and located in one place. This came to an end (or so I thought) when I moved on to my new professional life in New York City.

Then my interests changed to hearth and home and, in time, to the work of a single artist, Mary Frank, whom I had worked and played with. I came to own many works by Mary Frank, but I never, ever thought of myself as a collector. This was a dirty word in my lexicon. That is, until I was awakened by a friend who used the word "collector" when asking to see my Mary Frank's. The fact I had them all hanging in one place made my friend no less interested in seeing them, and made me no less a collector. But there was a difference. The art in my life had a driving emotional, sometimes disturbing force, unlike my stamps and travel books.

Given weekends at my home in Ulster County, it was only a matter of time before I came to know the historic Woodstock Art Colony. In college I had been not only a chemistry major, but an American history major as well. The first painting I bought was by a little-known Woodstock artist who played baseball with George Bellows. I focused on the work of Eugene Speicher and Bolton Brown, hardly knowing that each also had the strongest artistic and personal connection to George Bellows imaginable. Eugene Speicher was an athlete, student of Robert Henri, National Academy painter, and draftsman extraordinaire—renowned in his lifetime. Bolton Brown was a mountaineer, founder of the art department at Stanford University, co-founder in 1902 of the Byrdcliffe arts and crafts colony in Woodstock, and father of modern art lithography in America—virtually forgotten in his lifetime.

It was only later that I discovered Speicher was neighbor and best friend of George Bellows and Brown was Bellows' lithographer of choice, printing the majority of Bellows' lithographs and co-signing, as fellow artist, each that he printed for Bellows. Yes, I knew somewhat of Bellows' boxing images, but at that time I knew much more about Speicher and Brown than I did about Bellows. In time this changed as I discovered, through my interest in the historic Woodstock Art Colony, the breadth, depth, vision, power, and passion of Bellows across different media, in particular his lithographs.

I learned about the *War Series*, and with the passing of time this came for me to symbolize for me Bellows' honesty, brilliant draftsmanship, and his view of life, violence and brutality included. That Bellows had never been in combat or in Europe (just as Bellows knew nothing about boxing) made it all the more interesting. Add to this that the *War Series* represented the single most sustained effort in his career; he died early (at age 42) before a full life; the *War Series* opened in New York in 1918 to unexpected acclaim; in addition to the War Series he had done (usually with Bolton Brown) loving, sensitive portraits of his family and friends; and last but not least, there was little interest in the *War Series* when I began collecting them. These taken together were the ingredients for me, a confirmed contrarian, that allowed me to acknowledge being a "collector" with pride and with barely a hint of negativity to that word.

I think about today. Perhaps there is an artist who will give visual expression to the horrors now unfolding in the written reports of Serbia and Kosovo. Will that artist capture for posterity that unspeakable war as Bellows did with the *War Series*? We now have tele-vision, but these are sound bites and fleeting images. Nothing brings emotion and horror home in such concentrated fashion as the lithographs of the *War Series* do. You judge for yourself. You may find that artist—and be a collector.

Arthur A. Anderson
Morgan Anderson Consulting
New York City

Introduction

George Bellows and the Conflicts of his age

George Bellows did not become a printmaker until 1916. He had arrived in New York City from his hometown of Columbus, Ohio in the fall of 1904 to study painting. Over the next decade he rapidly gained acceptance as one of the most promising young artists of what became known as the Ash-can school of art. He and his peers painted all aspects of contemporary life including the less fortunate and downtrodden of society. Bellows' signature paintings dealt with the boxing ring. Perhaps his most famous and enduring work was the 1909 oil painting entitled *A Stag at Sharkey's*. This work depicted two semi-professional boxers slugging it out in a makeshift boxing ring in the rear of a rowdy saloon owned by Tom Sharkey on Manhattan's West Side. *A Stag at Sharkey's* was a thoroughly modern painting. Its subject matter, for its time, pushed right to the edge of what was suitable for public viewing. The work was painted in bold strokes of oil paint, broadly applied, but not so loosely as to destroy the illusion of a three-dimensional scene.

In 1913 artists and society in America were exposed to new trends in painting being promoted by the great masters of European art. In that year was held the famous International Exposition of Modern Art at the Armory of the 69th Infantry in New York. Often referred to as The Armory Show, this grand exposition showcased the new abstraction that heretofore had not existed as a relevant consideration for painting. Prior to this time artists could paint within a broad range of techniques, but ultimately their finished work had to represent in two dimensions, a three-dimensional illusion of a recognizable subject. The abstract modern art coming from Europe and shown at the Armory dismissed the primacy of illusion as the purpose of fine art. In other words, the content or message of painting no longer could be found solely in the illusion portrayed. The form of painting gained ascendancy. How the painting was made, or in essence created, was a worthy enough goal of art.

The advent of abstraction in painting called into question the legitimacy of American painting. Artists such as Bellows had to decide whether or not their work had validity. Many of Bellows' peers struggled with this new debate of where art was going. They had not fully defined the purpose of their art prior to 1913. The message of their art, that had been intuitively defined, seemed lost and outdated. In contrast to the majority of artists, Bellows redoubled his efforts to send out a clear message in his art. This he did primarily by becoming a printmaker. Between 1916 and 1917, Bellows completed over forty different lithographs. Many of these images were inspired by earlier paintings. The lithograph, *A Stag at Sharkey's*, of 1917 followed closely the painting from twelve years before.

A Stag at Sharkey's, (illus. p. 7), at its most basic level, is about violence. Because the boxers are professionals, the bludgeoning that is occurring is often overlooked. Instead, the viewer sees the beauty of the sculpted physiques and is awed by the power of their blows. One should not make the mistake though, to think that Bellows was unaware of the brutality portrayed. He recognized that he was no expert on pugilism. In his own words, he said, "I don't know anything about boxing. I'm just painting two men trying to kill each other." Moving away from sports, the artist was not hesitant to expose the often-rapacious nature of man. Two prints, *The Old Rascal* (no. 1) and *The Hold-Up* (no. 2), reveal the true nature of unavoidable confrontation. In *The Old Rascal* aggression and fear confront each other. The nakedness of the woman leaves little doubt as to her vulnerability if not her acceptance as vanquished. *The Hold-Up* shows just as well the damaging violation of an individual. The helplessness in the victim's eyes when confronted by a gun is only magnified by the bodily intrusion of the pickpocket.

Bellows lived in a small townhouse in New York surrounded by his family—a caring wife, two children and his in-laws. Yet, he well understood the devastation that certain families endured when alcoholism infected a household. *The Drunk* (no. 3) shows the depth of his feelings. A first glance focuses on the physical struggle between an inebriated father and his wife and older daughter. Closer inspection sees the mental anguish of these three participants. Digging still deeper, one's eyes move to the left and see the absolute fright on the faces of the two young children cowering in the bedclothes. It is difficult to keep looking at the print because the scene is so shocking in its honesty.

Bellows had no qualms about describing scenes of individual tragedy. He showed little restraint in his portrayal of man's response to violence. To him the judgment of a criminal was often as harsh as any crime that could have taken place. *Electrocution* (no. 4) reduces killing to a barbarous act, no more humane than putting a gun to an individual's head. In *The Law is Too Slow* (no. 5) the victim receives the swift, though questionable, justice for a murder that he may or may not have committed. The lynchers are masked, not necessarily hiding their identities, but almost as revelers at a masquerade. The unfortunate victim is portrayed

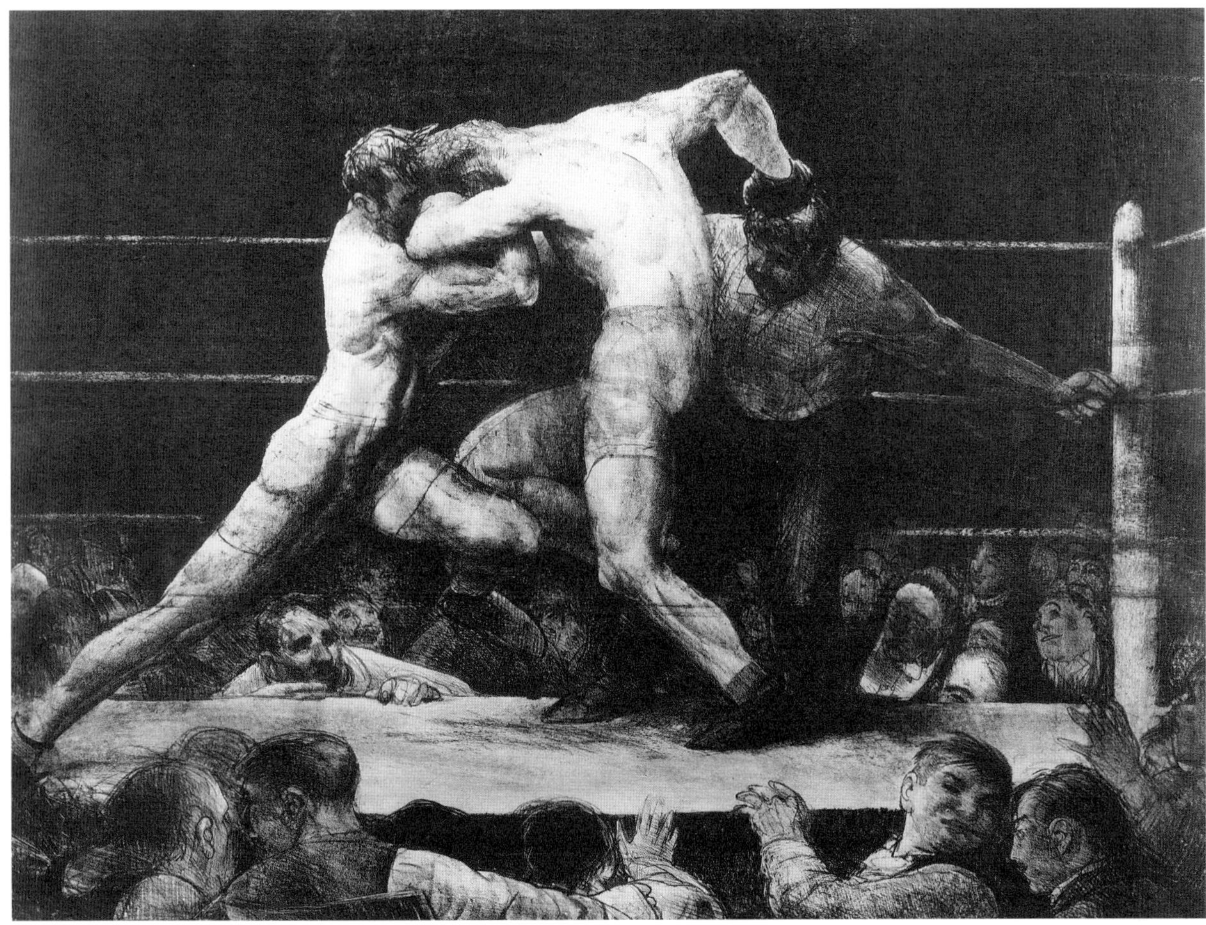

A Stag at Sharkey's, 1917
lithograph
18 ¾ x 23 ¾ inches

as a true martyr, being burned to death much like a saint of early Christendom. Religion and its iconography obviously had meaning to Bellows. After all, he grew up in a Methodist household and his middle name was Wesley, after the founder of this protestant sect.

Benediction in Georgia (no. 6) takes a caustic view of reform and the inappropriateness in Bellows' eyes of thoughts of salvation being preached to the helpless. How the crowd of inmates ended up incarcerated has no consequence except to indicate a one-way decline in humanity. Their lives don't necessarily consist of physical abuse, but of mental indifference to their true plight.

While scenes of domestic violence and societal abuse appear sporadically in the artist's work, there came a point, specifically in 1918, when he decided to focus all of his energies on the creation of studies in painting and prints of the greatest atrocities of his age—those that occurred during the Great War, or World War I. Like many Americans, Bellows had opposed his country's entry into the war. Once we decided to enter the fray in April 1917, however, there was no denying the reality of the situation in Europe. Hundreds of thousands of Europeans were killed between 1914 and 1917, regrettably, not just professional soldiers, but tens of thousands of innocent citizens. After America joined the war effort, Bellows volunteered for the Tank Corps. He was never sent abroad and was never part of the fighting. His interest in the war grew with his reading of the Bryce Report and the installment series by Brand Whitlock, America's Minister to Belgium, in Everybody's Magazine entitled "Belgium: The Crowning Crime." The serial specifically dealt with the atrocities committed by the German troops invading and then holding the country of Belgium. The first installment was published in February 1918. The Bryce Report was an accounting of the German invasion of Belgium in August 1915 based on over twelve hundred eyewitness accounts. It was published in abridged form in the New York Times on May 13, 1915. In the spring of 1918 Bellows began his series of lithographs dealing with the invasion. He used both of these written descriptions of war as a guide for his artistic depictions. He spent more than eight months completing twenty lithographs, thirty related drawings and five large-scale oils that make up the *War Series*. Whitlock used two of the lithographs, *Murder of Edith Cavell* (no. 10) and *Return of the Useless* (no. 20), in fact, as illustrations for the ninth and eleventh installments of his article on Belgium.

The fourteen war-related lithographs in this exhibition can be broken down into three general categories. The first grouping consists of three images of the battlefield. They include *The Charge* (no. 7), *Sniped* (no. 8), and *Base Hospital* (no. 9). *The Charge* shows the aftermath of hand-to-hand combat on the front line. Dead bodies litter the landscape. This is a scene that has been repeated over and over again in the history of war. *Sniped* focuses on individual suffering and is just as powerful as the preceding work because it makes us one with the circle of compassionate military personnel. *Base Hospital* concludes this trilogy with the humane effort of saving lives injured in the course of fighting. While tragic, these scenes of war are easily accepted. They conform to the generally acknowledged understanding that death and physical harm between professional killers are inevitable under the rules of engagement.

The second threesome deals with the capture and treatment of military prisoners. *The Murder of Edith Cavell* (no. 10) tells the story of the execution by the Germans of the British Red Cross head-nurse, who was accused of aiding in the escape of prisoners from her hospital in Belgium. Bellows portrayed her as a heroine, at the top of a flight of stairs, making a grand entrance, much as an actress entering the stage. The moment is almost surreal, coming shortly before her tragic end in front of a firing squad. *The Case of Sergeant Delaney* (no. 11) continues the glorification of the POW. Although Delaney's future is anything but hopeful, he stands resolute and powerful before his oppressors. *Gott Strafe England* (no. 12), the German words for "God punishes," gives the first glimpse of the more horrific aspects of the treatment of captured soldiers. Gone is any semblance of honor between combatants. The defeated are damned to an ignoble death and the victor reduced to the role of a savage.

The last category consists of the largest group of prints and represents Bellows unique contribution to our understanding of the "Great War." They deal with the inhumane treatment of the innocent citizenry as opposed to the scenes of traditional conflicts in war. Two of these eight lithographs, *Village Massacre* (no. 13) and *The Barricade* (no. 14), centered around groups rather than individuals. In the first, the citizens of both genders and of all ages are caught in the midst of the throws of slaughter. Some already have been shot, while others grieve in their final moments before death. *The Barricade* reduces the crowd to nothing more than three-dimensional amorphous shapes. Stripped of their clothing, they lack identity and have become effective shields against bullets and bayonet strikes.

Bellows elicits an even stronger response from us when he makes us confront the plight of the individual. In *The Germans Arrive* (no. 15) a young man has had both hands cut off by his adversaries. There is no escaping the terror in his eyes and the emotions running through his head. Until recently, this type of barbarism seemed far-fetched. Recent acts of similar maiming in Africa reaffirmed the truth of man's capacity to commit such atrocities. Bellows takes this savagery to its ultimate nadir in *The Bacchanale* (no. 16). The only true innocent ones are children. Here they are impaled on bayonets and foisted in the air. There is no escape from the recognition that these soldiers were truly depraved. Women, regrettably, are often the unfortunate victims of war. Before death they are often subjected to rape and mutilation at the hands of their captors. In three telling prints, *Belgian Farmyard* (no. 17), *The Cigarette* (no. 18), and *The Last Victim* (no. 19), Bellows narrates in graphic detail the dismal fortunes of so many nameless women. In the first, rape has already occurred. The woman is left for dead, while her attacker calmly gets dressed. The contrast between the perpetrator and his prey is even more pronounced in *The Cigarette*. The mutilated body of the young woman with breast removed and outstretched hand impaled to the door are almost impossible to look at, but the nonchalance of her aggressor forces us not to look away. The artist allows us no freedom from our outrage. In many ways the explicitness of *Belgian Farmyard* and *The Cigarette* give greater weight to *The Last Victim*. One can only imagine her ultimate fate and hope that death will come quickly.

The final lithograph in the series on World War I was most likely *The Return of the Useless* (no. 20). Bellows sets the scene aboard a converted cattle car where Belgian citizens who had been forced into German work camps were returned to their homeland, broken both physically and spiritually. The transport of the impressed laborers has eerie similarities to the movement of concentration camp victims of World War II. Bellows worked hard on this series of the war. He leads us to recall the often-quoted adage that history must be remembered or it will repeat itself. Hopefully we will learn from his imagery.

Glenn Peck
H.V. Allison & Co. NY

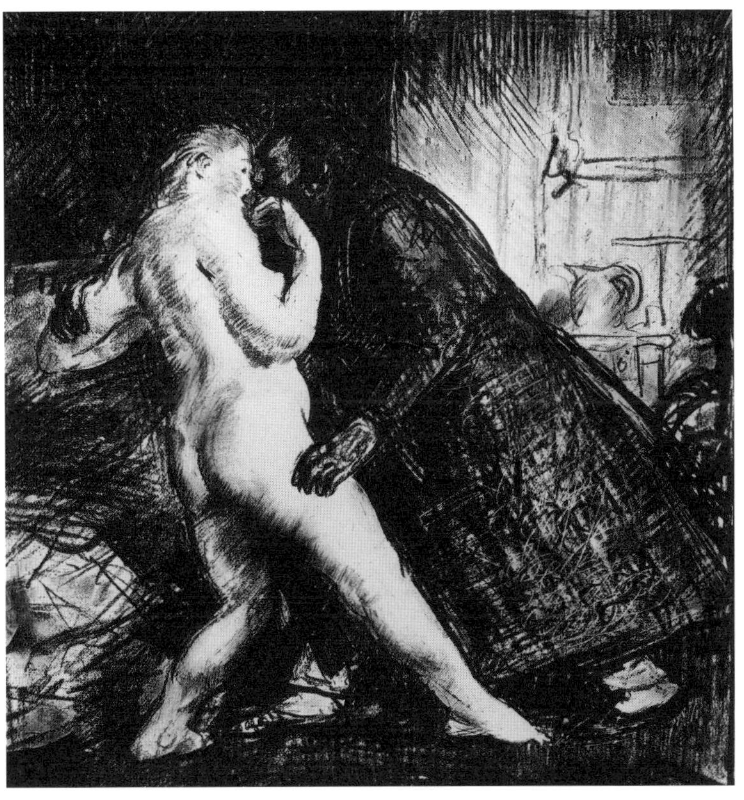

1. *The Old Rascal,* 1916

A certain ambiguity exists surrounding this image. The only reference Bellows made about this print was that he was inspired by the ribald writing of the 16th-century French satirist Francois Rabelais. Clearly though, there is an underlying unease in the scene. The buffoonery of the older man's advances is overshadowed by the trepidation evident in the eyes of the naked young woman.

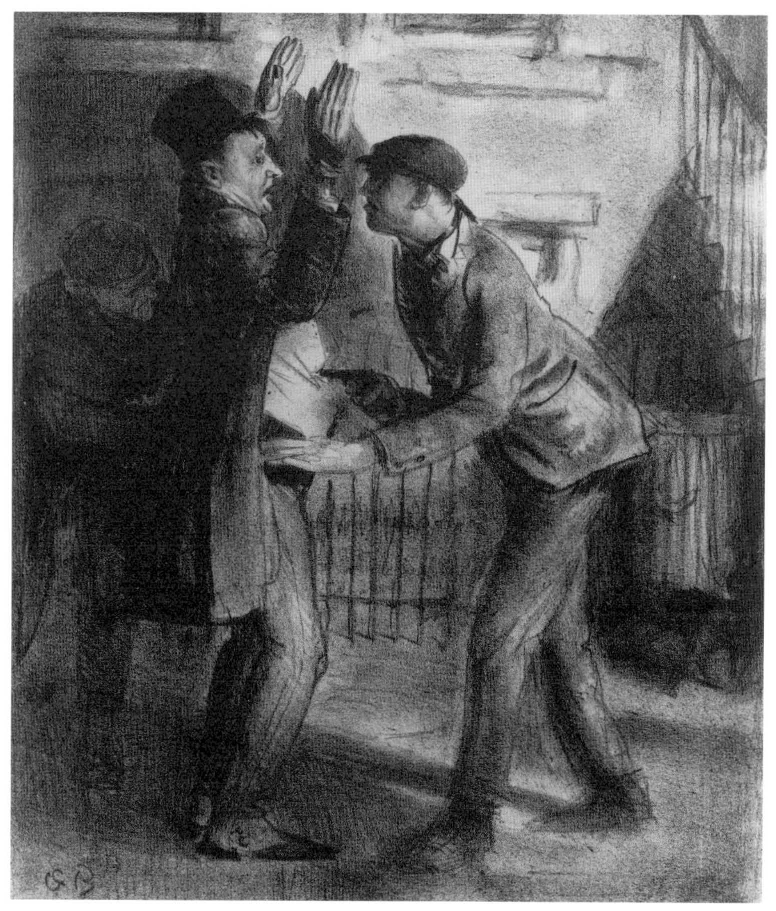

2. *The Hold-Up,* 1921

Bellows did two states of this print. In the first and present state, the pickpocket is clearly visible behind the man being robbed. The artist darkened the entire scene in the second state, sacrificing the pickpocket, for a more ominous atmospheric effect.

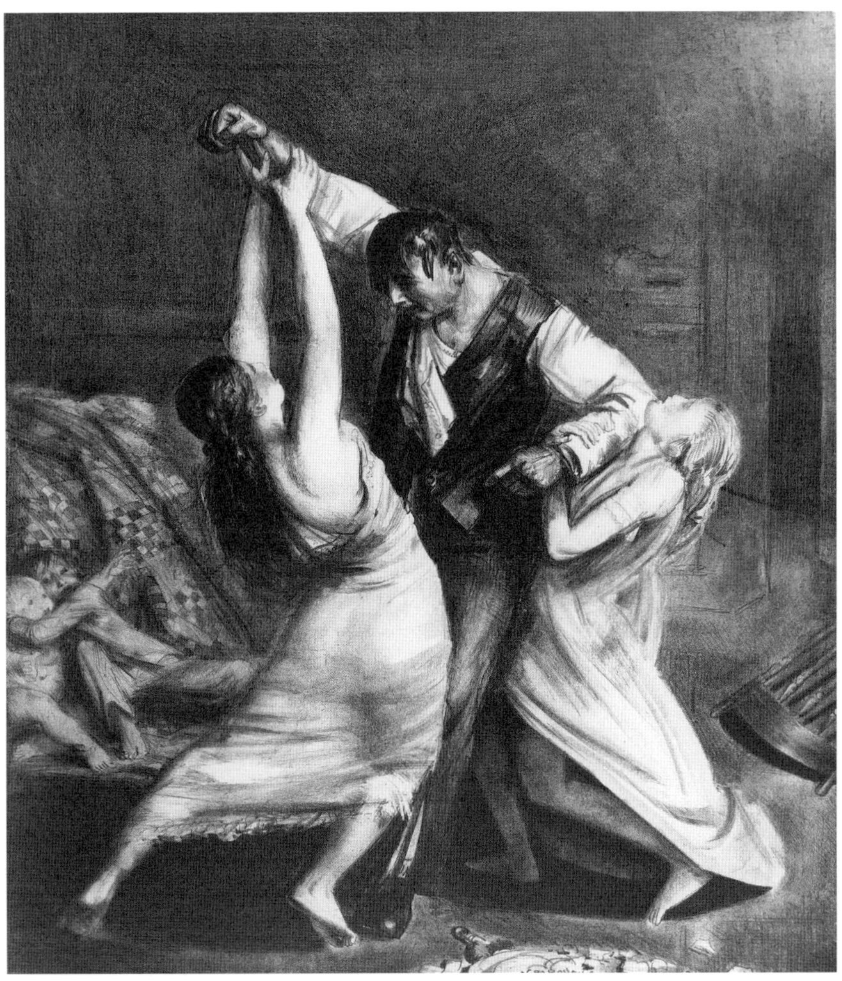

3. *The Drunk,* 1923-1924

Two different versions of *The Drunk* exist. The first stone had the mother's right breast exposed, but Bellows decided that this sent the wrong message. He was more concerned with the psychological struggle of alcoholism than dealing with sexual violence in this image.

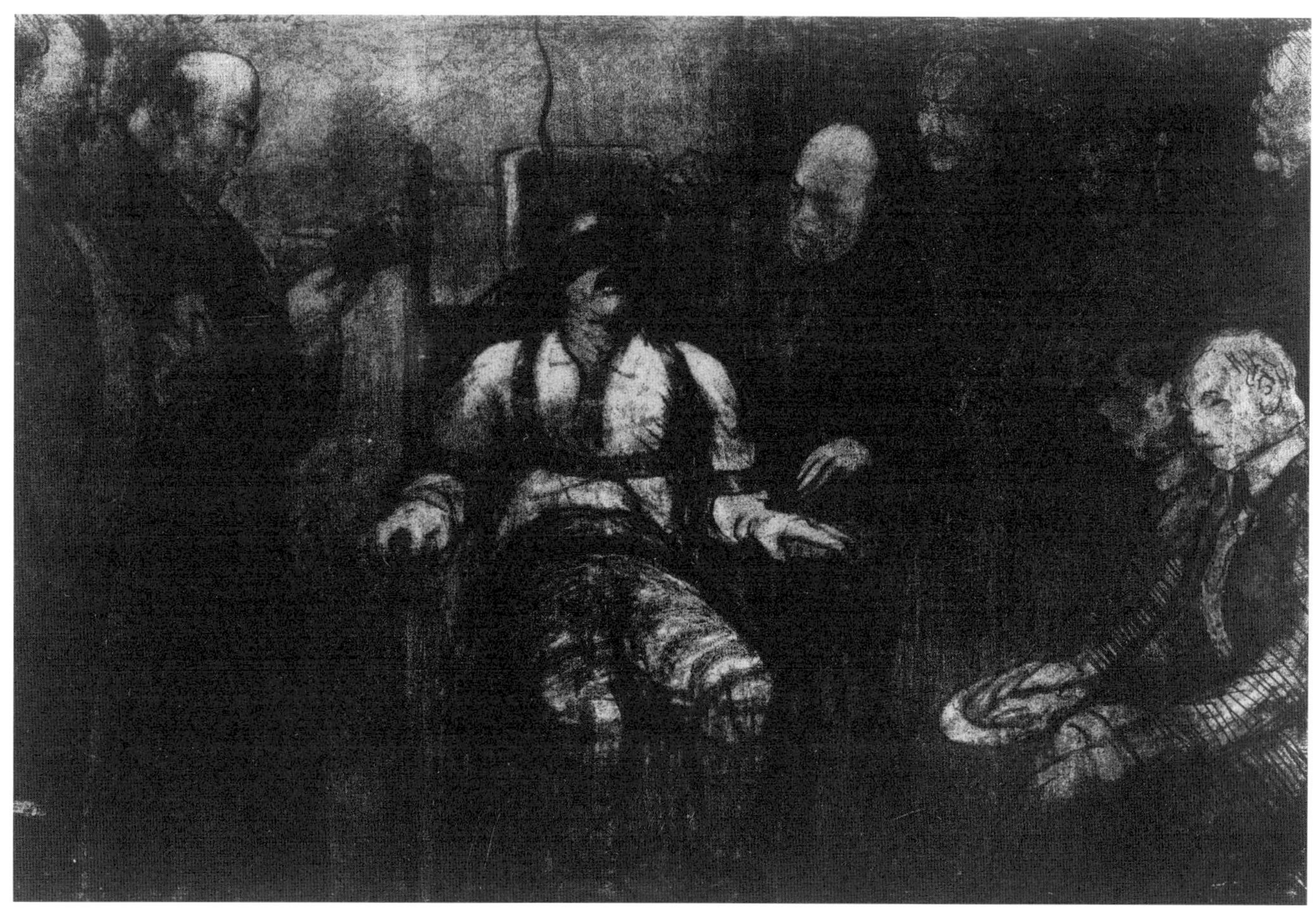

4. *Electrocution,* 1917

The artist considered capital punishment to be one of the most horrible phenomena of contemporary society.

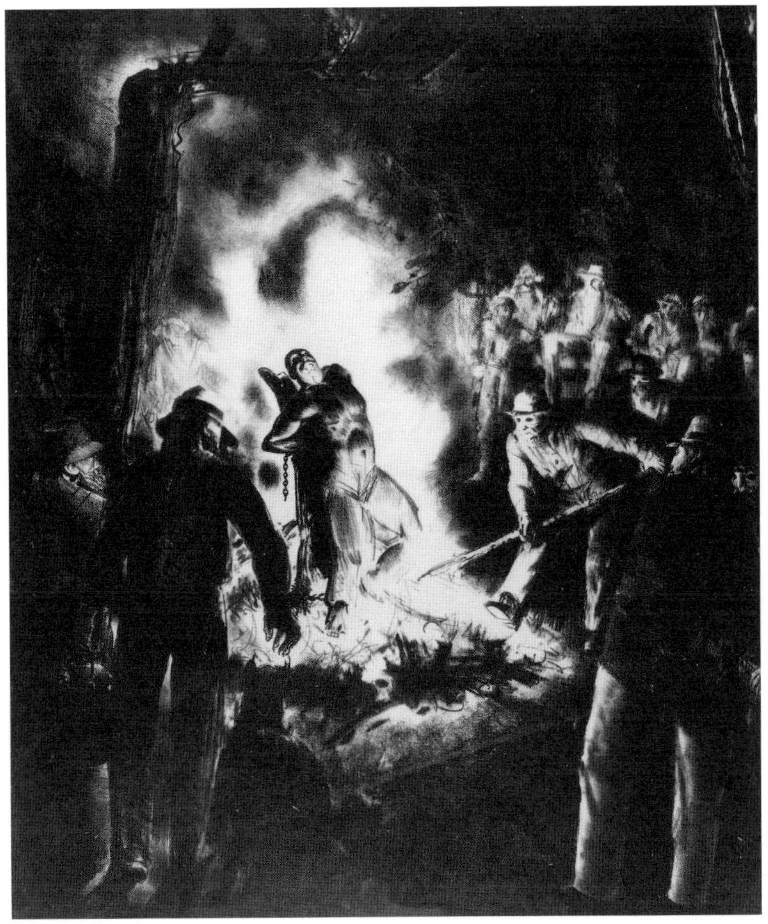

5. *The Law is Too Slow,* 1923

Of all Bellows illustrations for short stories that appeared in the periodicals of his day, this is the most poignant characterization of the racial tensions that existed at that time. It served as an illustration for Mary Johnston's story "Nemesis" that was published in Century magazine in May 1923 and documented the lynching of a black man for the supposed murder of a white woman.

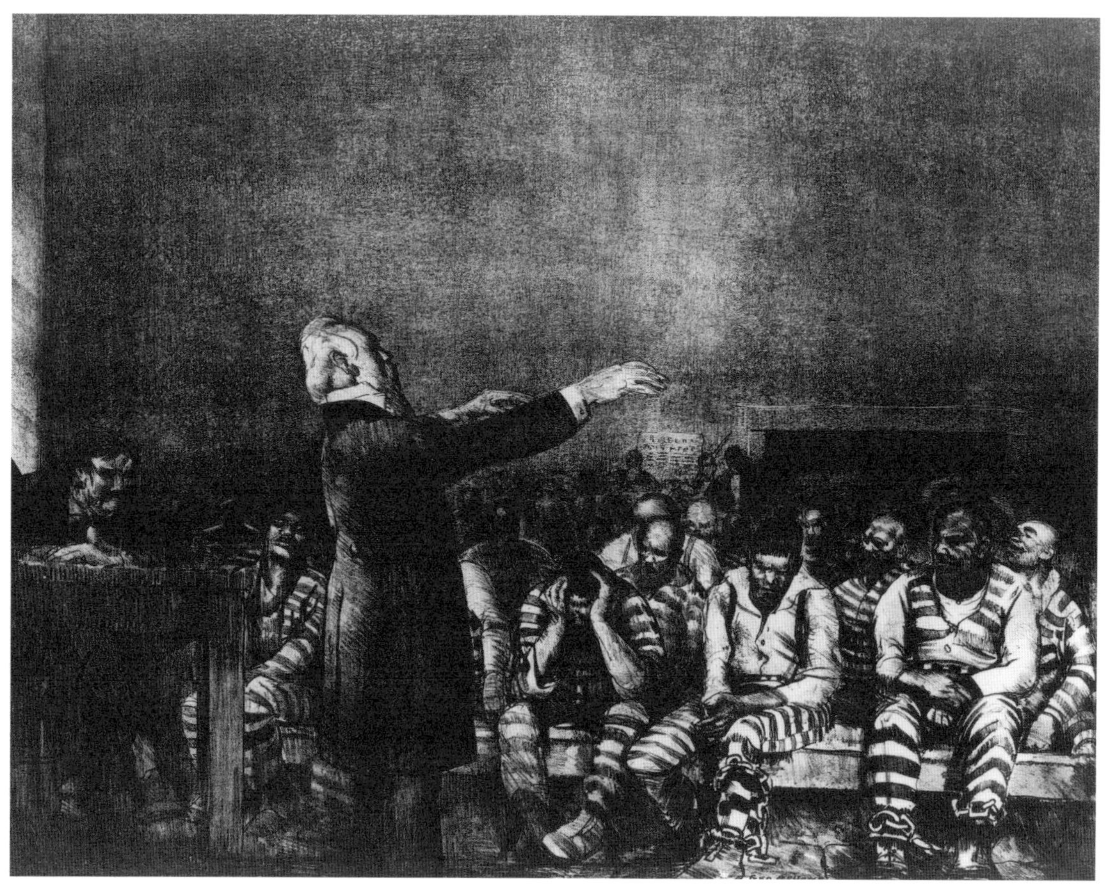

6. *The Benediction in Georgia,* 1916

Between 1911 and 1917 the most controversial magazine in America was The Masses. This magazine solicited articles and independent illustrations critical of society's ills. Of continued interest was the hypocrisy prevalent in race relations. Bellows was a regular contributor to this magazine and submitted this image for reproduction in May 1917.

War Series

At the 1919 exhibition of his lithographs held at the Albert Rollier Art Galleries in Chicago, Illinois, George Bellows included twelve prints under the heading "War, Subjects Founded on the Bryce Report." The Bryce report was an eyewitness account of the atrocities that the German armies committed during their invasion of Belgium in 1915. Bellows wrote the following introduction:

> *In presenting the pictures of the tragedies of war I wish to disclaim any intention of attacking a race or a people. Guilt is personal, not racial. Against that guilty clique and all its tools, who organized and let loose upon innocence every diabolical device and insane instinct, my hatred goes forth, together with my profound reverence for the victims.*

Bellows wrote a brief statement for each lithograph. His comments appear in italics below the relevant reproduction.

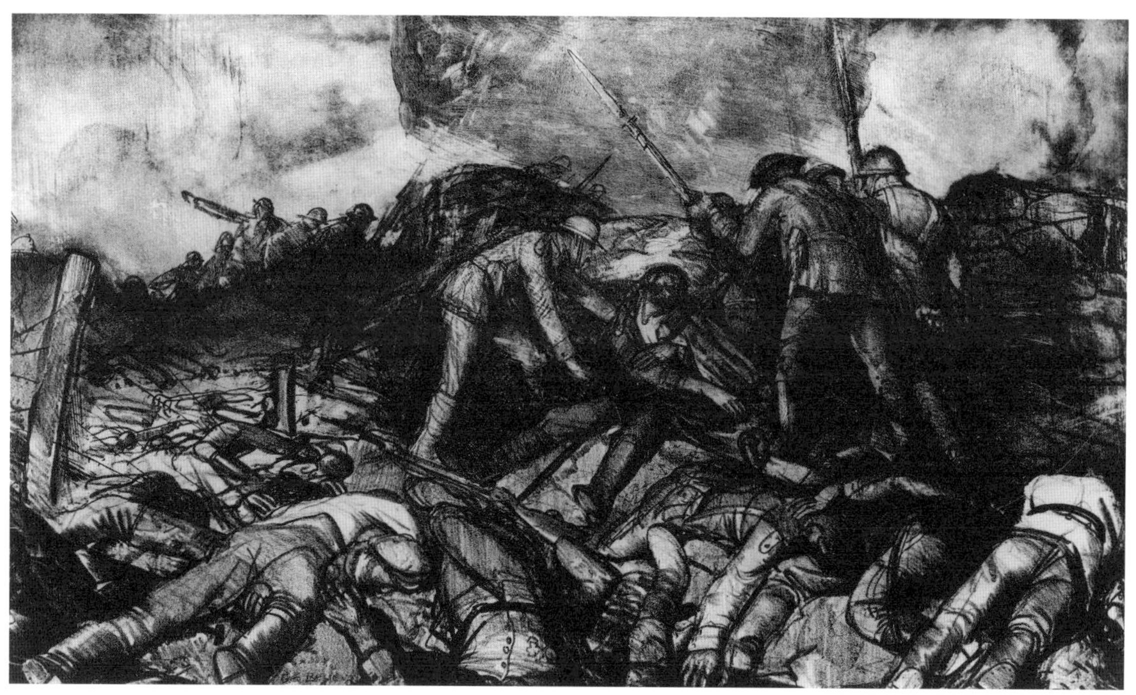

7. *The Charge,* 1918

The Charge appeared as an illustration for Donal Hamilton Haines' short story about field combat in France in Collier's, July 13, 1918.

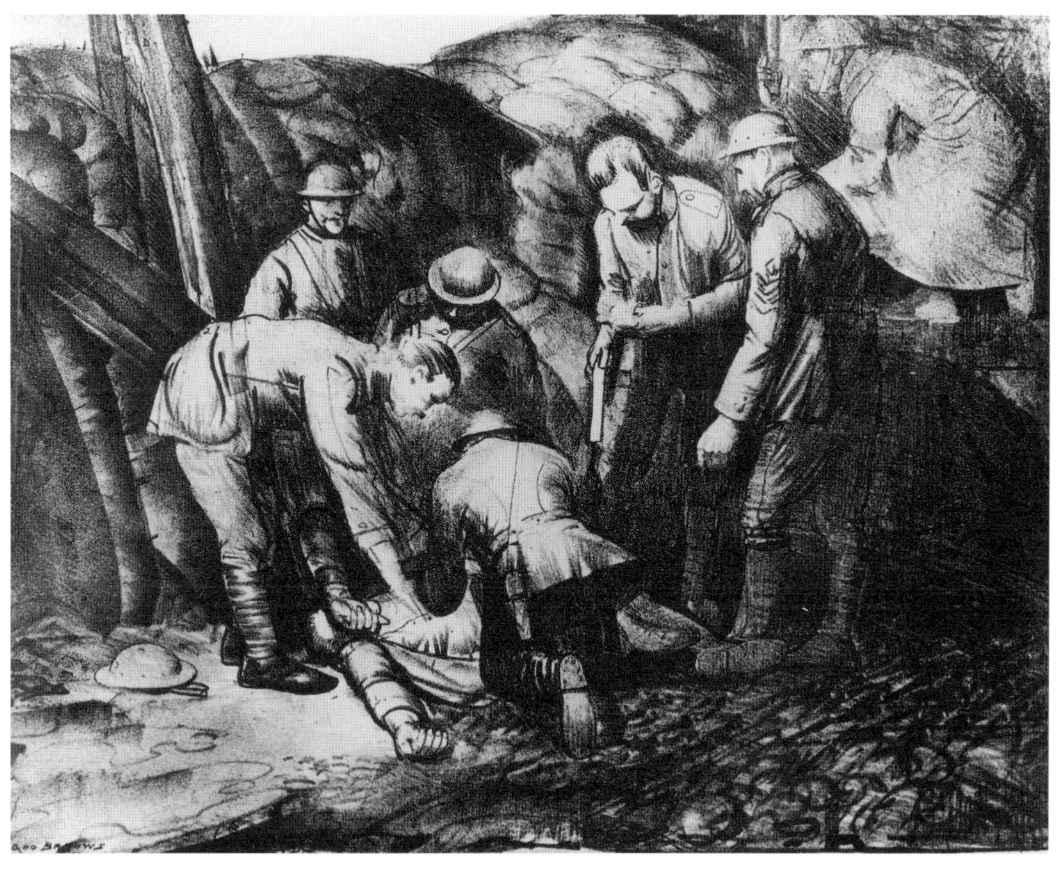

8. *Sniped,* 1918

Study of soldiers binding the wounds of a victim of German snipers.

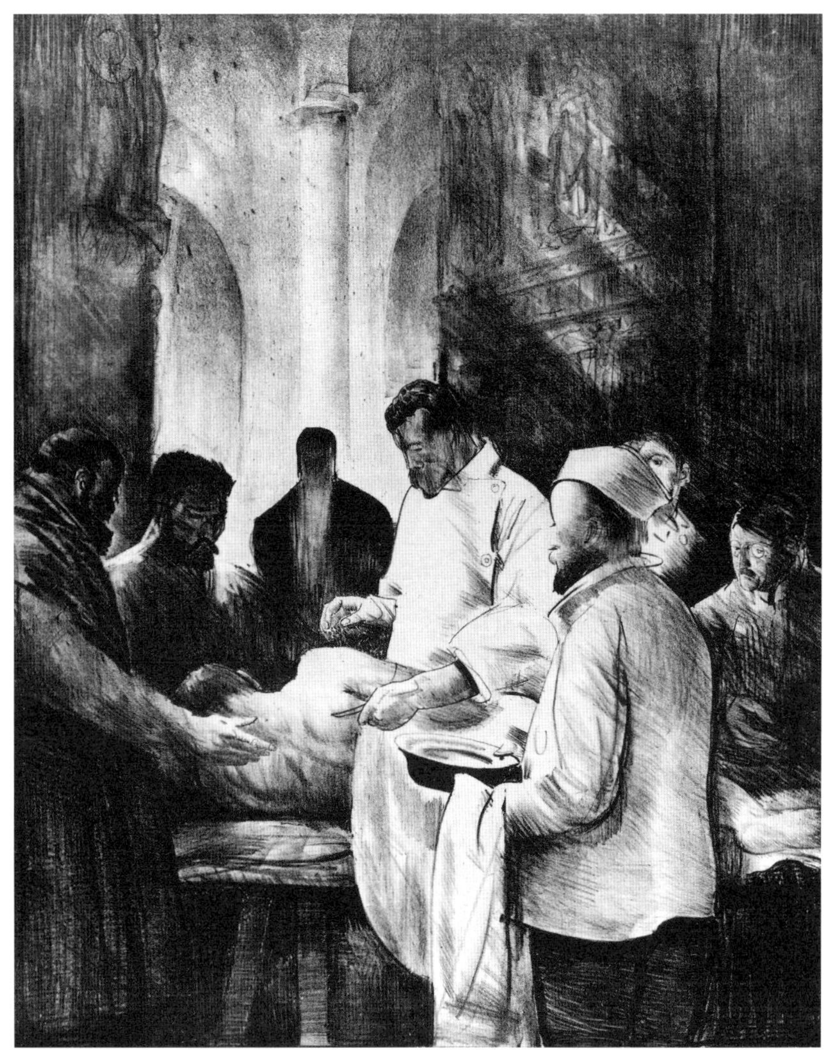

9. *Base Hospital,* 1918

Study of a doctor's clinic at a dressing station in a cathedral. An effort to see what could be done with photographs as material.

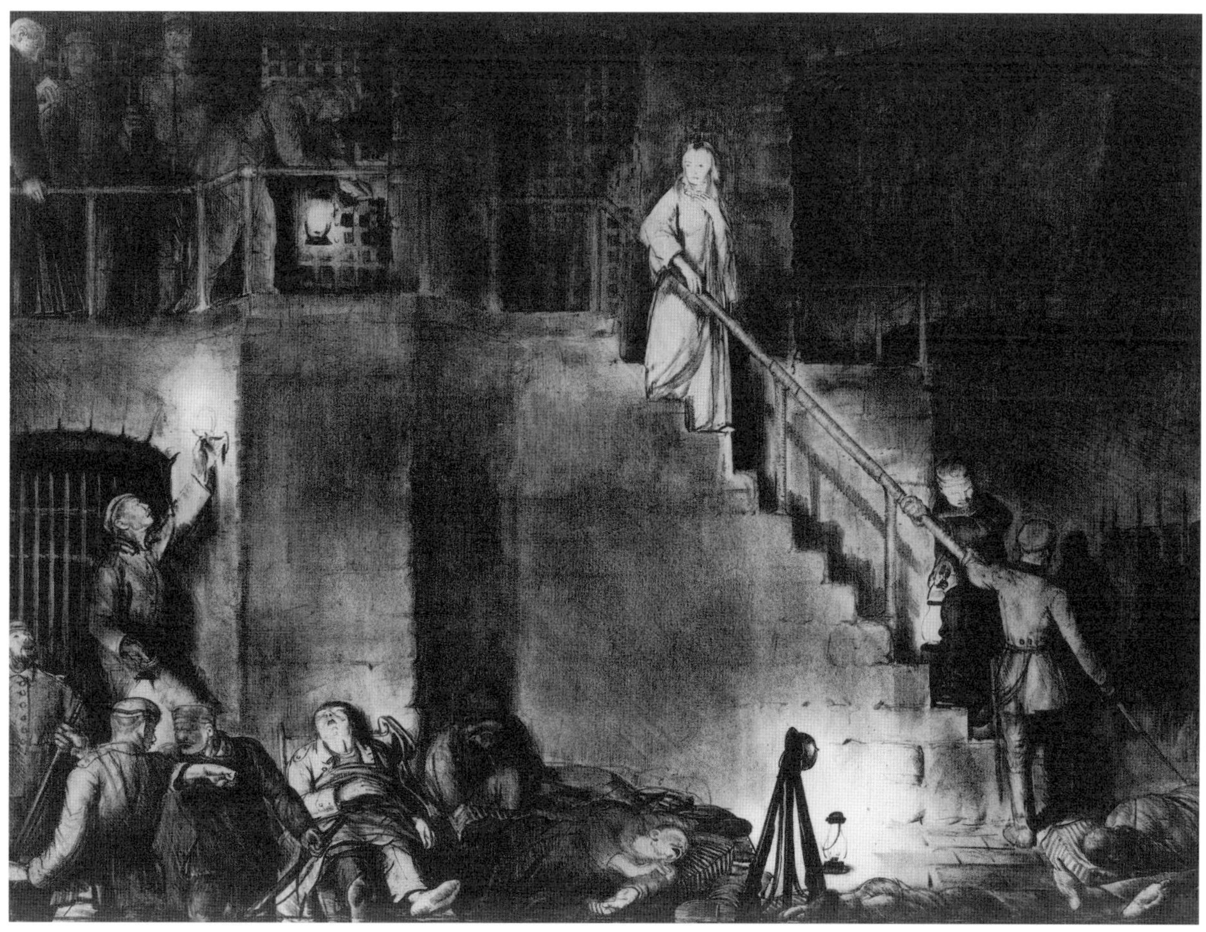

10. *Murder of Edith Cavell,* 1918

Little material is available at present about the precise conditions of her execution. She was aroused at 2 a.m. with no time allowed for dressing. She appeared in her wrapper unattended except by the regular prison chaplain at the military prison of St. Giles.

Edith Cavell was a British Red Cross nurse in charge of a military hospital in occupied Belgium. She was accused of helping Allied troops escape and was executed by firing squad on August 12, 1915. When Bellows published this print the scene needed no introduction since Cavell was a famous tragic figure of her time.

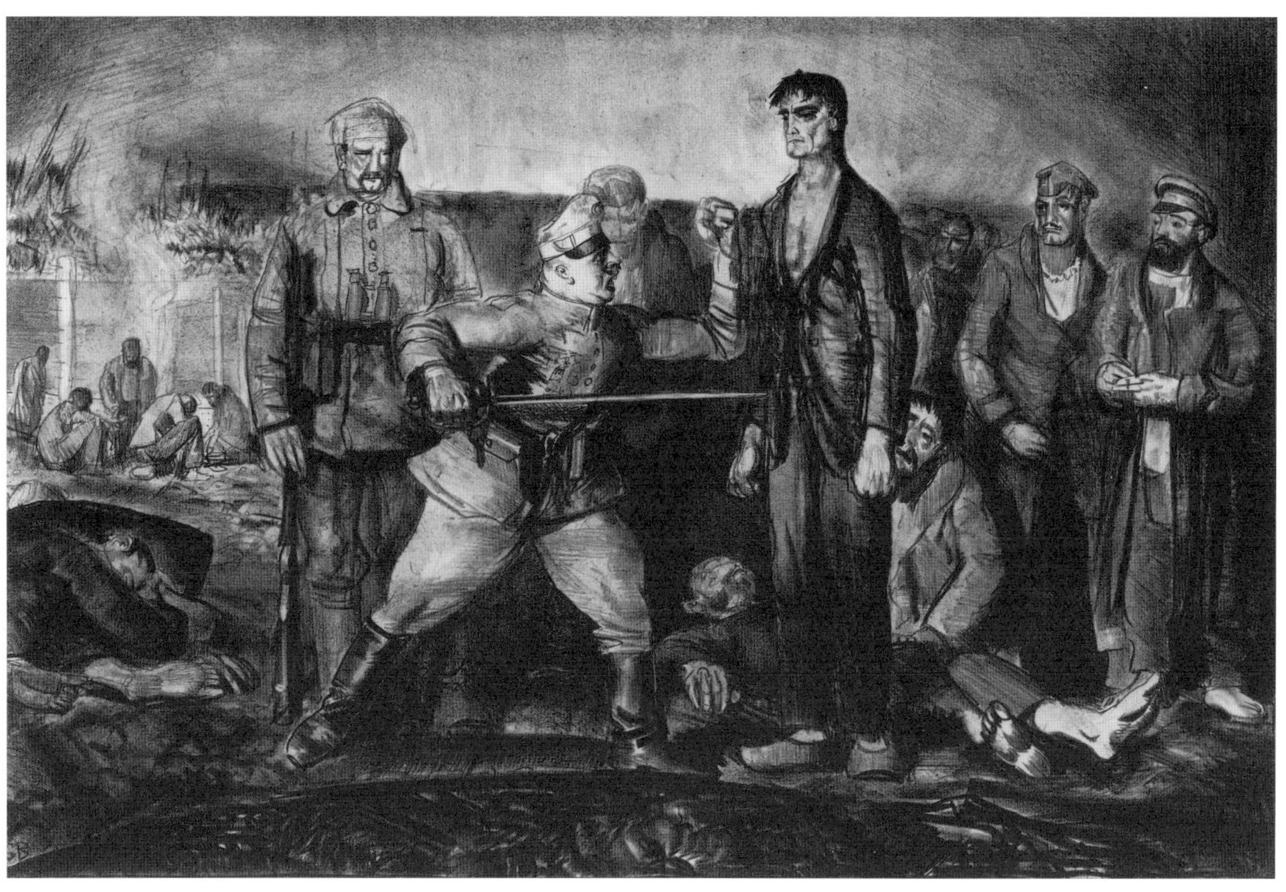

11. *The Case of Sergeant Delaney,* 1921

Little is known about *The Case of Sergeant Delaney* except that Bellows created it as a piece of post-war propaganda for the U.S. Navy.

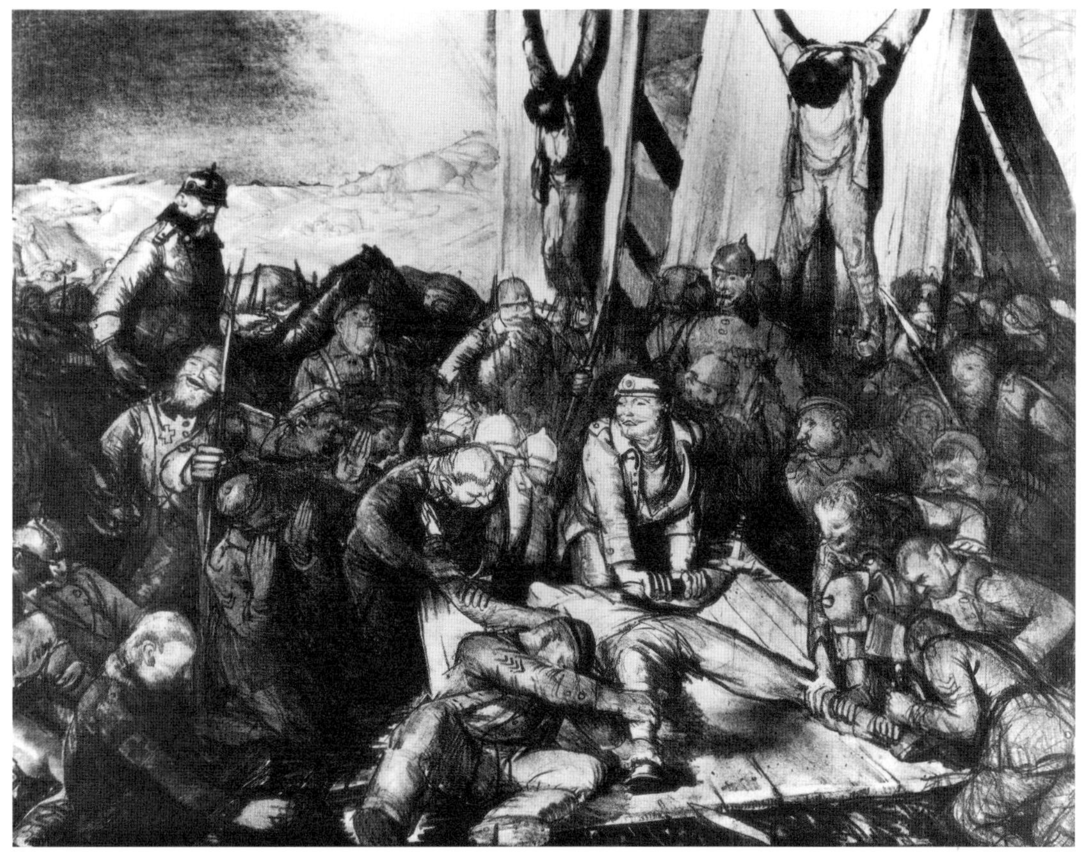

12. *Gott Strafe England,* 1918

Three British Tommies nailed to doors.

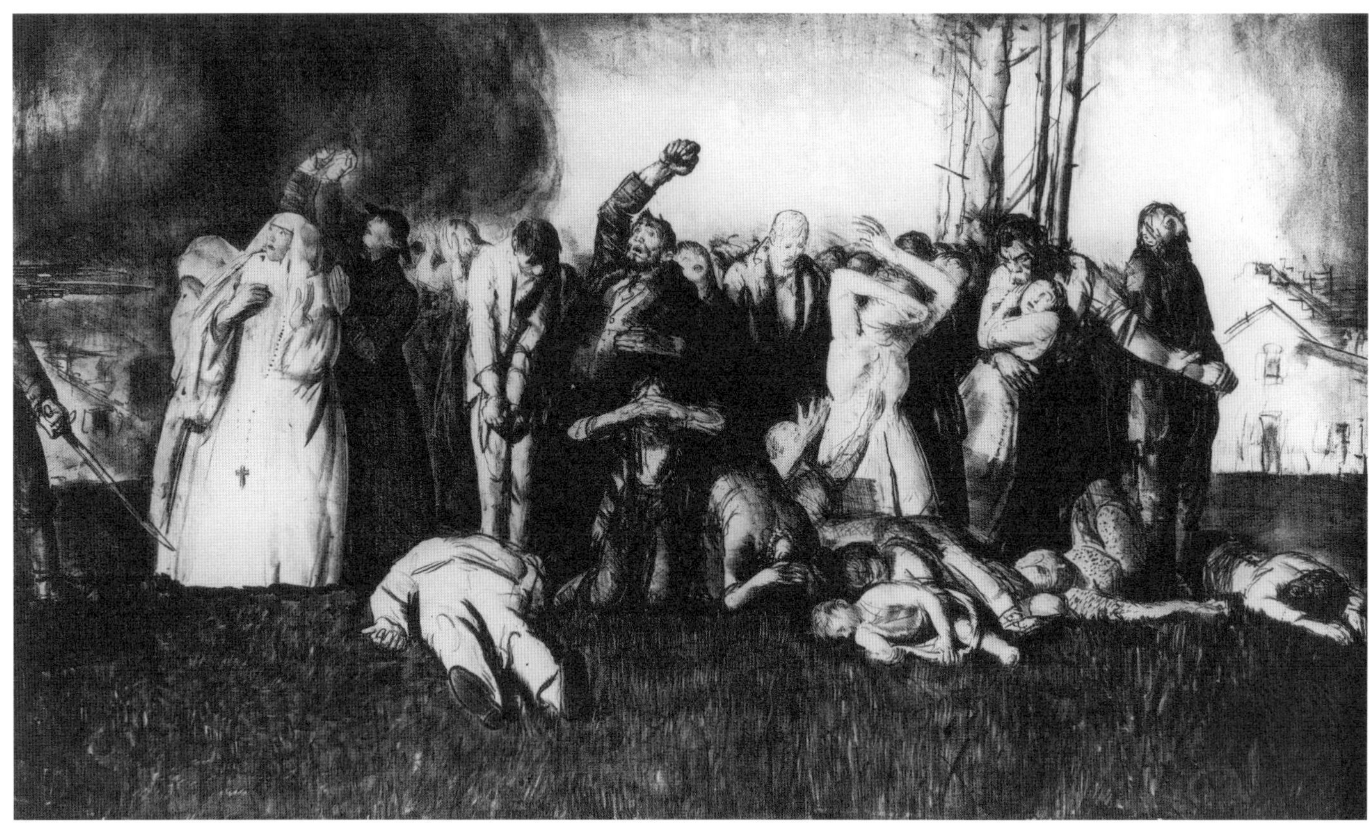

13. *Village Massacre,* 1918

At Dinant there were from five to six hundred civilians massacred singly and in groups. This lithograph, unaltered, is used as a motive for the painting *Massacre at Dinant*.

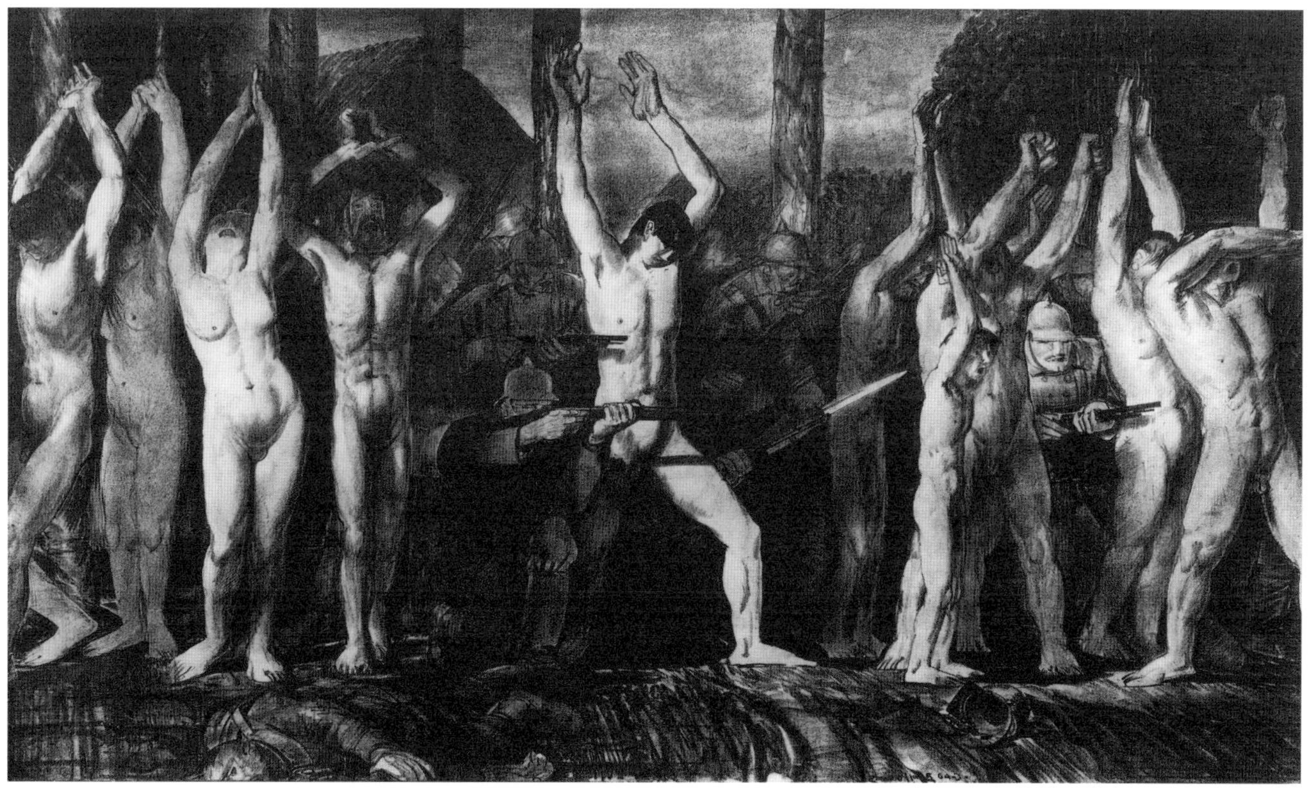

14. *The Barricade,* 1918

Belgian civilians in at least one instance were stripped and marched in front of the troops as a shield.

Originally Bellows drew *The Barricade* on the lithographic stone with the riflemen appearing left-handed. This occurred because he forgot that during printing the image drawn on stone would appear as its mirror image. He redrew the entire composition in reverse so that it would print with the riflemen as right-handed.

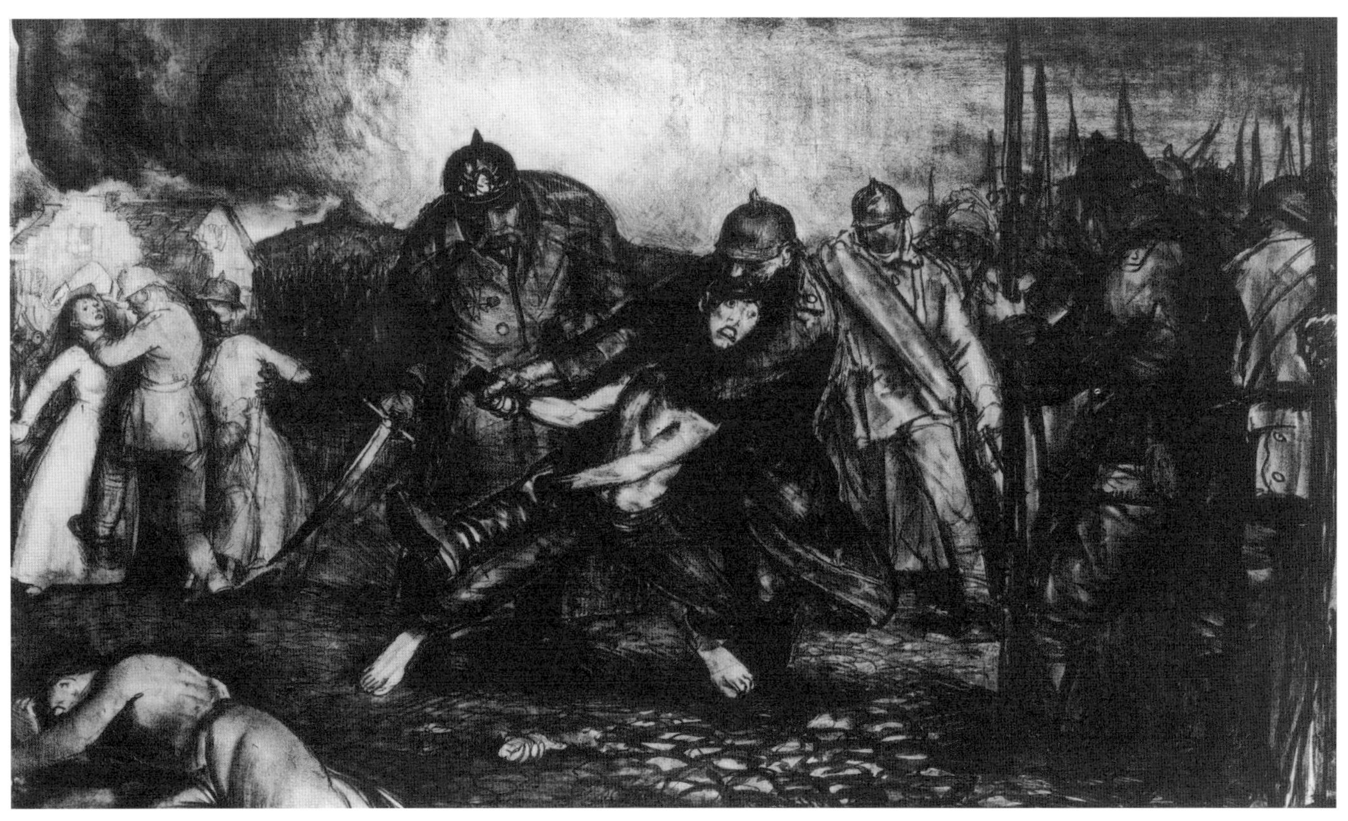

15. *The Germans Arrive,* 1918

Drawn for the Liberty Loan. Study for a painting.

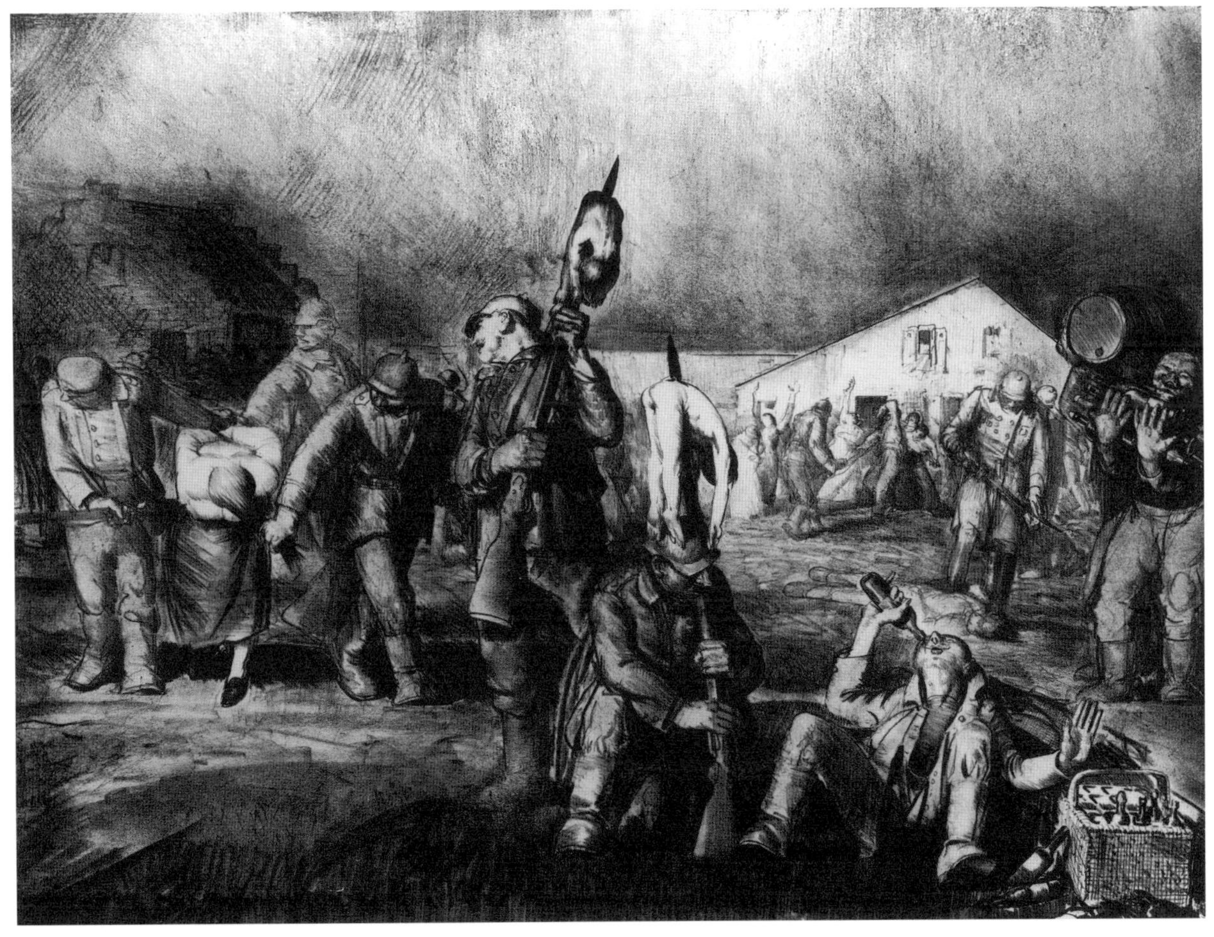

16. *The Bacchanale,* 1918

The German soldiers marching through Belgium were encouraged to commit outrages. The impaling of children on bayonets was common according to many eyewitnesses.

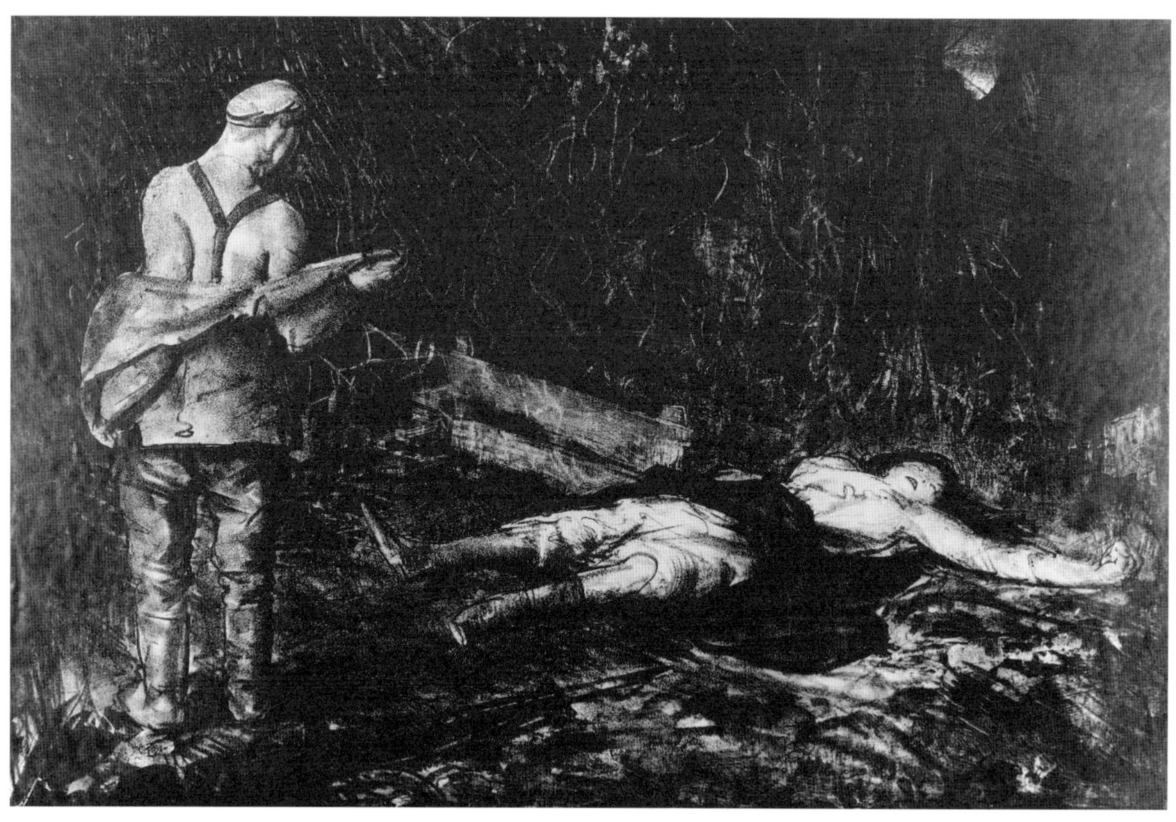

17. *Belgian Farmyard,* 1918

The eternal crime when the animal is let loose.

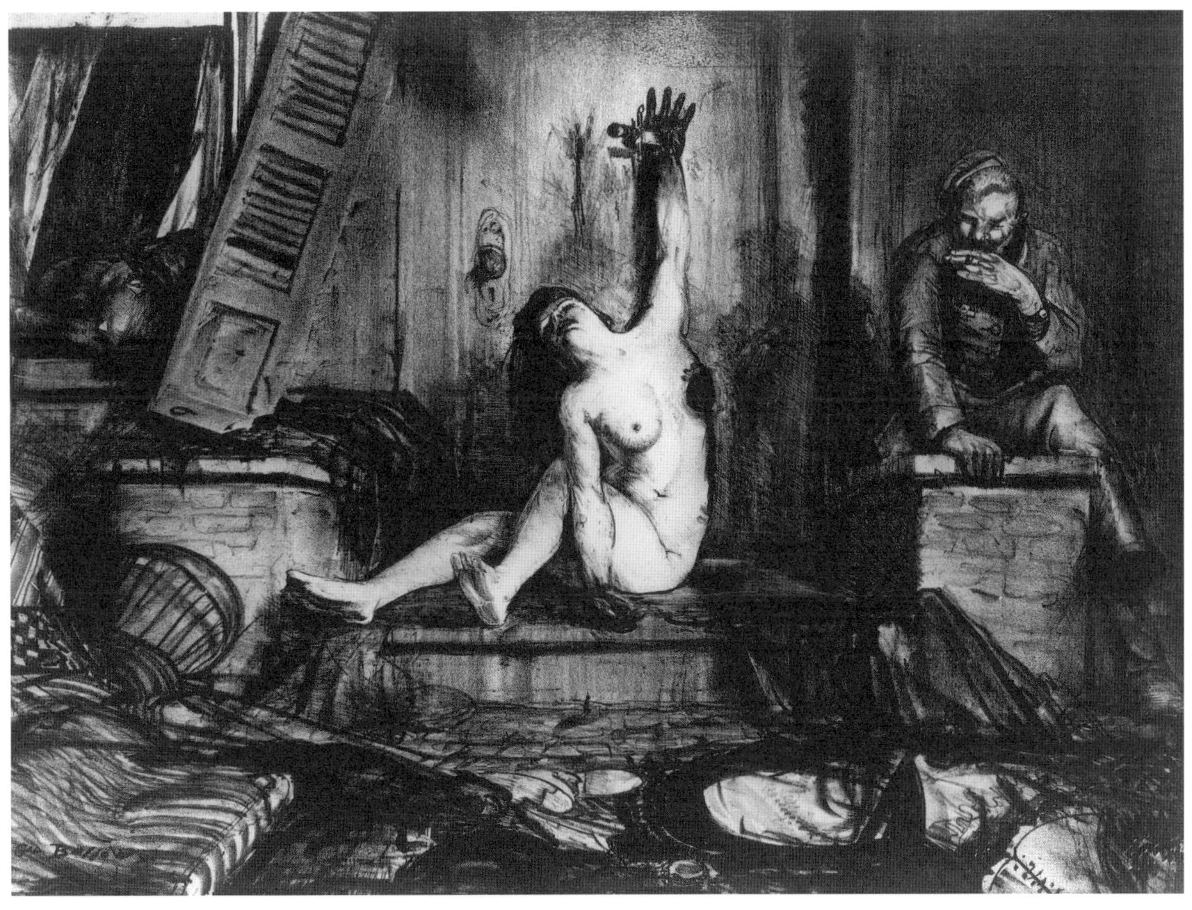

18. *The Cigarette,* 1918

Mutilated woman stripped and impaled to a door. A lieutenant smokes on the door step. The Bryce Report has much testimony about events of this character.

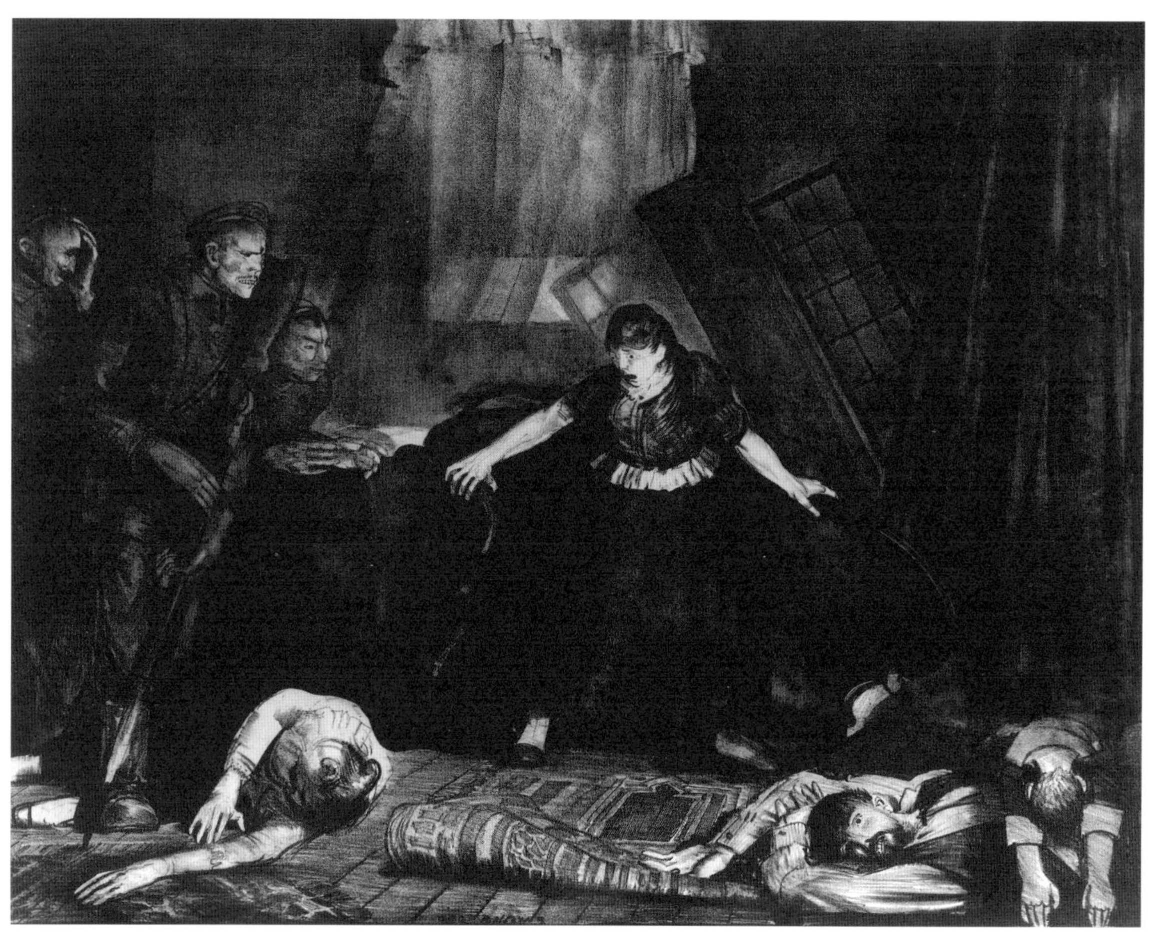

19. *The Last Victim,* 1918

German soldiers enter a pleasant home during the wild first passage through Belgium. They kill mother, father, brother and have a further inspiration about the girl. Incidents of this character were wholesale according to the official evidence.

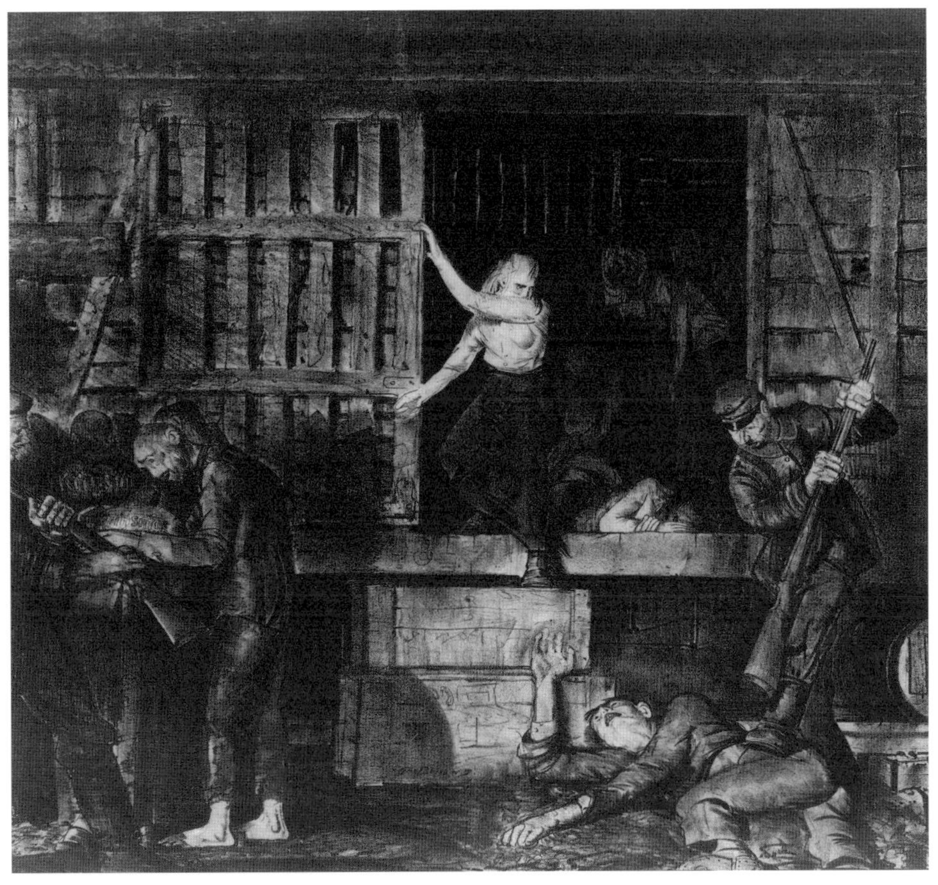

20. *The Return of the Useless,* 1918

Belgian slaves being shipped back and dumped, broken in health and useless for further exploitation by their German masters.

Works in the Exhibition

All works are original lithographs on paper and are courtesy of Morgan Anderson Consulting, New York City. Dimensions refer to image size and are in inches; height precedes width. Parentheses indicate alternate titles.

1. *The Old Rascal,* 1916
10 ⅛ x 9
Edition: 53

2. *The Hold-Up, First State,* 1921
11 x 8 ½
Edition: 42

3. *The Drunk,* 1923-24
15 ⅝ x 13
Edition: 35-50

4. *Electrocution, Second State*, 1917
(Electrocution, Large)
(Electrocution, Small)
8 ⅛ x 7 ½
Edition: 51

5. *The Law is Too Slow,* 1923
17 ⅞ x 14 ½
Edition: 26

6. *Benediction in Georgia,* 1916
16 ⅛ x 20
Edition: 80

7. *The Charge*, 1918
(The Russian Charge)
10 x 16 ¼
Edition: possibly 50

8. *Sniped,* 1918
8 ⅞ x 11 ⅛
Edition: possibly 50
War Series

9. *Base Hospital, Second Stone,* 1918
24 ¼ x 19 ¼
Edition: unknown
War Series

10. *Murder of Edith Cavell*, 1918
(Edith Cavell)
18 ¾ x 24 ¾
Edition: 103
War Series

11. *The Case of Sergeant Delaney,* 1921
(Delaney)
(The Incident of Sergeant Delaney)
17 ¼ x 25
Edition: possibly 30

12. *Gott Strafe England*, 1918
(God Punishes)
(Gott Strafe)
15 ⅜ x 19 ⅛
Edition: possibly 50
War Series

13. *Village Massacre*, 1918
(Massacre)
(Massacre at Dinant)
17 ¾ x 29 ⅝
Edition: possibly 80
War Series

14. *The Barricade, Second Stone,* 1918
(The Barricade, No. 2).
17 ⅛ x 28 ½
Edition: possibly 50
War Series

15. *The Germans Arrive,* 1918
(The Enemy Arrive)
(Made in Germany)
15 ¾ x 25 ⅞
Edition: possibly 70
War Series

16. *The Bacchanale, Second Stone, Second State,* 1918
18 ⅜ x 24
Edition: possibly 50
War Series

17. *Belgian Farmyard,* 1918
13 x 18 ¾
Edition: possibly 50
War Series

18. *The Cigarette,* 1918
14 ½ x 19 ¼
Edition: possibly 50
War Series

19. *The Last Victim,* 1918
18 ⅞ x 23 ⅜
Edition: possibly 20
War Series

20. *The Return of the Useless*, 1918
19 ⅞ x 21 ½
Edition: possibly 72
War Series

State University of New York
New Paltz